SMART BRAIN RIGHT BRAIN

An Introduction to Forms of Art

Om KIDZ
An imprint of Om Books International

1. Forms of Art

Throughout history, the rise of many great cultures and civilisations has depended on how well advanced they were in the arts.

The first paintings, from the Stone Age, were found on cave walls

The Egyptians painted elaborate scenes on the walls of pyramids and temples

Art forms comprise Literature, Visual Arts and Performing Arts.

Literature includes Poetry, while Cinema and Multimedia are part of all three arts. Visual arts are Painting, Sculpture, and Architecture.

Music and Dance are Performing Arts.

Through arts, an artist shows or shares their ideas, imaginations and emotions.

In performing arts, the artist, also known as the performer, performs these arts in front of an audience. According to each performing art, the artists, or performers, are also known as musicians, dancers, singers, poets, actors, and directors.

2. Painting

Painting has been an important part of human life from the ancient cave paintings to the graffiti of today. Some of the best-known artists, like Michelangelo, Leonardo da Vinci and Edgar Degas, for example, were painters.

Michelangelo

Leonardo da Vinci

Edgar Degas

DID YOU KNOW?

The first paintings were cave paintings. Ancient people decorated the walls of caves using paint made from dirt or charcoal mixed with water or animal fat. They also blew paint through hollow bones just like spraying painting.

What is painting?

Painting is using colours to create art. We use many kinds of paints to make an artwork, like pencils, chalk, watercolours, acrylics, oils, and even charcoal.

What is the difference between drawing and painting?

Drawing has a single layer which is done with a pen or a pencil, and is the entire image. But in painting, one layer is painted over another layer, using crayons, colour pencils and paints, to get the final image. So, the image is not clear till it reaches the last stage.

POCKET FACT

Famous paintings created by famous artists are kept in big art galleries like the Louvre in Paris and the National Art Gallery in London.

A brief history of paint

Before linseed oil was used in paint, artists mixed dried pigments into egg yolk! World War II brought a change in the paint industry as linseed to make the paste was scarce. Artificial resins were invented and developed. These were cheap, durable and held colour well, making painting much easier. It was only in the 1950s that acrylic paint was available commercially.

DID YOU KNOW?

Oil paint takes as long as 12 hours to two weeks to dry. Why, some museum curators do not consider oil paintings to be thoroughly dry until several decades have passed! Acrylic paints dry between ten minutes to two hours.

What is digital painting?

Digital painting is creating a painting digitally. This technique makes digital art in the computer with the help of computer graphics software program using a virtual canvas and a virtual painting box of brushes, colours and other supplies.

POCKET FACT

Paintings can be classified according to their style, genre and their main object. Still life, landscapes, seascapes, abstract and pop art are popular genres.

3. Sculpture

Sculpture is a three-dimensional visual art, usually created using materials like clay, stone or wood. Sculptures are made in two ways. Either it is formed bit by bit into a particular shape and structure with a material like clay or it is chiselled and carved from a block of wood or a piece of stone.

Sculptures can be made with wood, stone or clay

Sculpture: A brief history

The earliest sculptures were made with bone, wood and stone. With the improvement in tools and technology, artists began using clay and bronze. Sculptures of bronze and other alloys improved with time and new techniques like lost-wax casting, plaster-mould casting and sand casting. Wood carving was dominant in medieval Europe just like stone carving was in Greece.

Different styles of sculptures

Stone Age sculptures

Stone Age sculptors carved humans and animals. South Korean figures carved on deer bone date to 38000 BCE. The oldest carving, the Lion Man of Hohlenstein-Stadel, a lion-headed human figure from Germany is of the same period.

Sumerian and Akkadian sculptures

The Sumerians and the Akkadians were the first Mesopotamian civilisations. Their sculptures had lifelike animal forms and human figures with large, expressive eyes.

Ancient Egyptian sculptures

The ancient Egyptians followed a set pattern in their sculptures. Buildings, heads and animals were portrayed from the side, with eyes and torsos from the front. The Egyptian statues had erect bodies and size was used to show status.

Classical Greek sculptures

The Classical period began in Greece in 480 BCE and is known as Greece's Golden Age with great sculptors like Phidias and Polykleitos.

Hellenistic sculptures

The Hellenistic period began under the rule of Alexander the Great. Sculptures now not only depicted royalty, but also the common people. Great works like *The Dying Gaul* and *Laocoön and his Sons* were produced.

Sculptures in South America

The Olmecs were one of the first civilisations in Central and South America and had an advanced style of stone sculpting. They are famous for their 9-feet huge stone male heads.

Sculptures in the Western world

Sculpting in the West began in ancient Greece, producing great masterpieces in the Classical period. The Middle Ages saw Gothic sculptures based on Christianity, and the Renaissance period saw famous sculptures being created, like Michelangelo's *David*.

POCKET FACT

Today, sculptures are being made in a way that they move with the wind or when touched.

4. Music

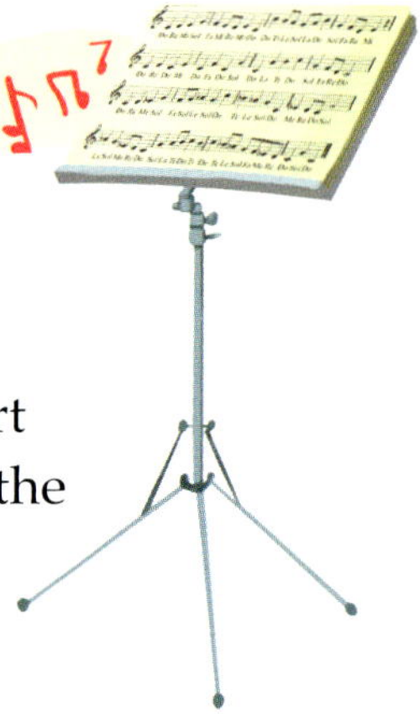

The word music comes from the Greek word (mousike), which means 'Art of the Muses'. In Ancient Greece, the Muses were the goddesses of music, poetry, art, and dance.

Music is sound organised by using rhythm, melody or harmony. Music is also vocal. People have been making music since the Stone Age. The first music was probably made by imitating the sounds and rhythms of nature. The first rhythm or percussion instruments were the clapping of hands, stones banged together, and other things that kept a beat. Each region in the world has its own music, for example, African music, Chinese music and Western music.

Do you know that mathematics and music are co-related. Numbers and math are often used to describe and teach music. For example, fractions are used in music to indicate how long the musical notes are.

DID YOU KNOW?

The famous composer Bach used the mathematical calculations of the 12th root of 2 so he could write better notes in his music.

Western music saw the classical period from 1750 to 1825 when composers like Haydn, Mozart and Beethoven made their mark in music. Everything became bigger, from orchestras to music pieces. The composers wrote longer pieces of music called **symphonies** with many sections called **movements**. Some movements were fast and loud, and some were sad and quiet. These composers often used a structure known as the **sonata** form.

Haydn

Mozart

Beethovan

Influence of Jazz

In the 1920s and 1930s, Jazz music influenced other types of music like blues, pop and rock music. Pop means any form of popular music. The 1950s saw rock and roll with Chuck Berry and Elvis Presley, and The Beatles became a famous pop music group in the 1960s. The 1970s saw other musical styles mixed with pop music, like soul and funk, for example.

DID YOU KNOW?

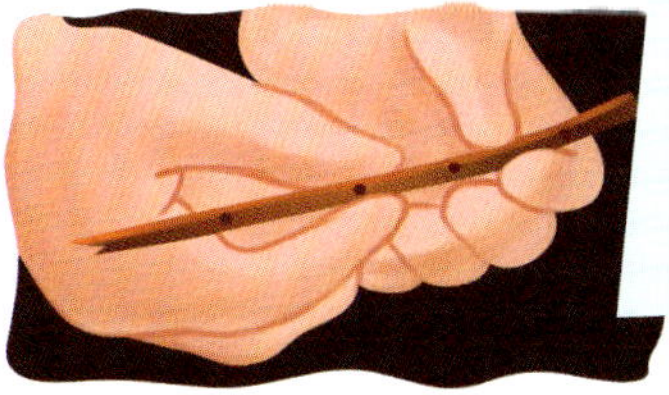

In 2008, archaeologists discovered a bone flute in the HohleFels cave near Ulm, Germany. This is the oldest musical instrument ever found.

5. Dance

People have been dancing for centuries to express their thoughts and ideas. Every human society has its own dances right from Asia to Europe to Africa. But the first evidence of dance comes from the 9,000-year-old cave paintings in India.

When people move to a musical rhythm, it is known as dance. Through dance we often celebrate occasions like independence, spring or a good harvest. People dance at weddings and sometimes at funerals too.

DID YOU KNOW?

The first known dance school opened in Paris in 1661 and only men could be members. It took them 20 years to realise their mistake. After 1681, women were accepted too.

Choreography

The planning of a dance is called **choreography**, and the person who does this is called a **choreographer**. Choreography goes with music and has a certain style.

POCKET FACT

A world record for the longest conga dance line was set by 119,986 people in Miami in 1988. Wow!

Popular dance from popular cultures

Put on your dancing shoes! Here's a collection of popular dance forms from all over the world.

- Some traditional dances have existed for hundreds of years. **Bharatnatyam** is a traditional Indian dance that has been passed down for centuries. Women perform the dance to pay tribute to the gods.

- The **polka** is a lively dance that originated in Central Europe. The polka dance was popular with young women.

- **Ballet** originated in Italy during the 1500s. This beautiful dance form is used to tell stories.
- **Capoeira** is an athletic Brazilian dance, combining dance with martial arts.

- Traditional Irish **stepdance** has fast, high steps and bright costumes.
- In the 1970s, **breakdance** was started in New York City by African American and Puerto Rican teenagers.
- Harry Fox invented the **foxtrot** in 1914.

- **Waltz** is one of the most popular dances today starting as early as the 16th century. But the first ballroom dance was the Italian Viennese Waltz.
- The famous modern dance the **Cha-Cha** originated in Cuba.

- The Greek dance **Epilinios** has dancers dancing on grapes and crushing them with their feet! Another Greek dance, the **Iporchima**, is used in theatres and combines dance and pantomime.

DID YOU KNOW?

The popular Greek dance Geronos is a rare dance in which only children dance together. No adults allowed!

6. Cinema

Cinema, also known as movies or films, uses moving pictures and sound to tell a story or help people to learn about something. People all over the world watch cinema as a form of entertainment. Some films make you laugh, and some make you cry or feel afraid. Cinema is shown in the big movie theatres and also on television. Recently, cinema watching has become popular on the internet.

How a film is made

At first, the screenwriter writes a script, which is the story of the movie and then writes the dialogues and actions that the actors will say and do. Then a producer hires people to work on the movie and organises the money that will be needed to pay for the actors and the equipment. Producers usually get the money by borrowing it from a bank or by getting investors to lend money for the movie production. The producer also hires a director to direct the movie who tells the actors what to do. The director is helped by the cameraman who takes motion pictures with a motion picture camera.

After the filming is finished, the editor puts the moving pictures together in a way that tells the whole story within a certain amount of time. Audio engineers and sound engineers record music and songs and join it with the moving pictures. When the movie is done, many copies of it are made by movie labs and put onto movie reels. Then the movie reels are sent to cinemas.

The movie is projected with a movie projector onto a large projection screen at the front of the auditorium while the dialogue, sounds and music are played through a number of loudspeakers.

Charlie Chaplin: A Hollywood legend

There have been many legends in cinema, but Charlie Chaplin is one of the greatest.

The multi-talented Charlie Chaplin was a British actor, comedian, movie maker, screenwriter, editor, musician, and author. He was famous for making silent movies (where there was no talking or sound). He acted, directed, scripted, and produced most of them.

Charlie Chaplin performed for almost 70 years, beginning when he was five years old, and finishing when he was 80. The character that Charlie Chaplin played most was called "the Little Tramp".

DID YOU KNOW?

In the year 1915, Chaplin took part in a Charlie Chaplin look-alike contest just to have fun. Surprisingly, he didn't win this contest but found himself in the third place.

7. Poetry

Poetry is an art form and also a part of literature. A poem can be written in a few words or be as lengthy as an epic poem. The epic is one of the earliest forms of poetry with lots of heroes and lots of actions.

The best poem shouldn't feel like a poem.

It should be like a good story instead.

Poems don't have to make sense;
They don't have to rhyme either.
They can be fun, or they can be difficult.
A good poem is the one you love.
The one you read again and again.
The perfect poem can make you smile for the good,
and weep for the bad.
It's like a song you sing,
And like a book you read.

As you can see, I didn't use rhymes in this poem, because while a good poem has rhyme and reason, the best poem can be written any way.

DID YOU KNOW?

The oldest poem is from Babylon. *The Epic of Gilgamesh*, the story of a king who is half-man and half-god is more than 4000 years old. The longest poem is from India. The epic Mahabharata has almost 1.8 million words.

Poetic forms

There are many forms of poetry like the sonnet, haiku, ballad, limerick, nonsense rhymes and nursery rhymes. It is also not necessary that poems should rhyme. Poetry is artistic writing that may be funny or serious.

The lines or group of lines found in a poem are called **stanzas**. A stanza normally has 12 lines. A two-line stanza is called a couplet and a four-line stanza is a quatrain. There are poems that follow strict rules. For example, the **sonnet**, an English form of poetry, has 14 lines of 10 syllables each. **Haiku** is a Japanese form of poetry with just three lines. The first and third lines have five syllables, and the second line has seven syllables. Here's an example of haiku.

There are poems like **free verse** that do not follow any set form or pattern, using rhythms that are like everyday speech.

21st March is World Poetry Day. Thanks to a great initiative by the United Nations Educational, Scientific, and Cultural Organisation (UNESCO) this day is celebrated to appreciate and support poetry and poets from all over the world.

8. Architecture

Architecture is a form of art as well as a science. It is used to design structures or buildings like a small house, to a large city. To design and build any great structure might be a scientific marvel, but a good architectural design is a form of art. The Ancient Egyptians built large temples and structures, like the Great Pyramids of Giza.

DID YOU KNOW?

20,000 to 30,000 labourers were used to build the Great Pyramid at Giza, which took 23 years to complete.

Classical Architecture

The Ancient Greeks and Romans created what is now known as **'Classical Architecture'.**

Classical Architecture always followed laws or rules strictly. Symmetry (balance) and proportion (keeping shapes in certain ways) were used. The Golden Mean was a rule that stated: When you are making a room, or any other thing, it is best to make the long side 1.6 times longer than the short side. Other rules in Classical Architecture determined how high the middle of an arched bridge was supposed to be. This, in turn, made clear how wide the bridge would be. These rules or laws were created after thousands of years of experience, have been passed down from generation to generation and still hold good today.

Architectural styles

Different architectural styles were created in China, Japan, Southeast Asia, Africa, Mexico, and Central and South America. In India, the architecture of palaces and stone carvings on temples stands out.

DID YOU KNOW?

The Great Wall of China was built over a period of 2000 years and millions of workers were employed to make it.

In Western Europe in the Middle Ages, Romanesque architecture was created, followed by Gothic architecture. Gothic buildings can be seen in many churches and castles and feature tall, pointed windows, domes and arches.

The Industrial Revolution took place in the late 18th century and machines made things cheaper and faster. The Second Industrial Revolution took place at the end of the 19th century, making steel even cheaper. Architects started building with metal and concrete to create marvels like the famous Eiffel Tower in Paris.

Buildings were now taller than ever before and came to be known as skyscrapers. People said goodbye to the traditional methods of architecture and this new architectural style that began in 1890 was named **Modernism**.

DID YOU KNOW?

The tallest building in the world is the Burj Khalifa in Dubai, UAE, standing tall at 2717 feet.

9. Multimedia

Multimedia means various forms of content like text, audio, graphics, animation and video and how they are combined and used to entertain or inform the audience. Multimedia is used in fine arts, entertainment, software services, video games and many other areas. Experts in multimedia are known as multimedia artists.

Multimedia art combines a large range of art forms. Many arts and crafts are brought together under one common umbrella like film, literature, performance, music and sound, drama, visual arts, or design.

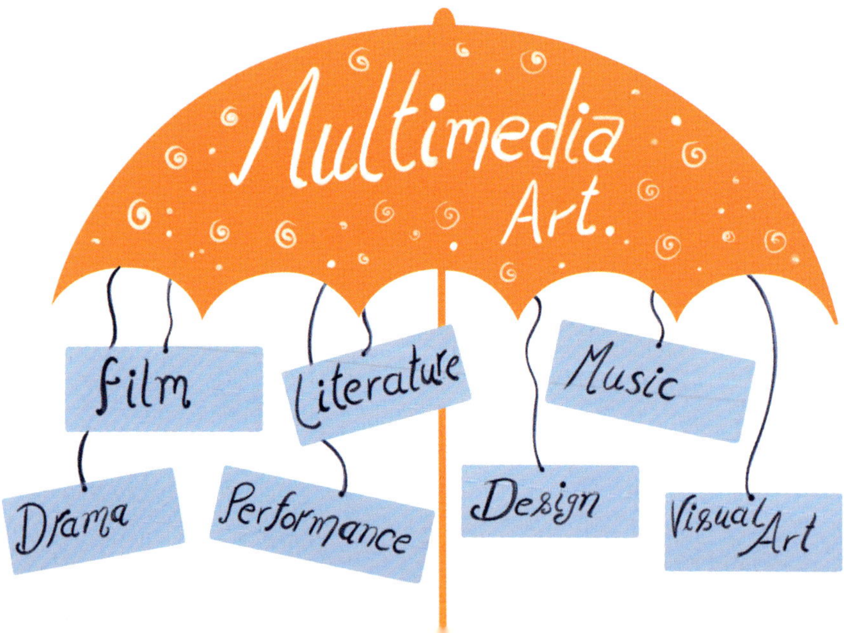

Multimedia art has become very popular in recent years. It is created with the help of technology. For example, an audio recording might play alongside a light display. A dancer might perform against the backdrop of a short film. A poem might use animated images. Multimedia games are also extremely popular.

Let's Get Active

Activity 1: The architect has made a big mess when he made these six houses. Can you help him by putting the halves of the houses where they belong?

Activity 2: Name the musical instruments given below.

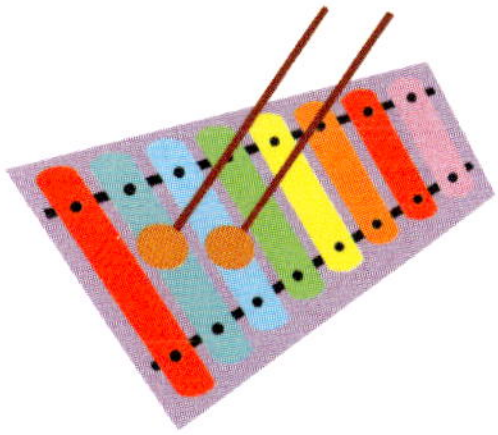

Activity 3: Match the definitions in Column 1 with the correct names in Column 2.

	Column 1		Column 2
1.	Three-line poem.	A.	Epic of Gilgamesh
2.	Tallest building in the world.	B.	Geronos
3.	Art created with the help of technology.	C.	21st March
4.	Oldest poem in the world.	D.	The Muses
5.	Inventor of the foxtrot dance.	E.	Burj Khalifa
6.	Goddesses of music, poetry, art, and dance.	F.	Haiku
7.	Greek dance only for children.	G.	Multimedia Art
8.	World Poetry Day.	H.	Harry Fox

GLOSSARY

Graffiti	words or pictures that are written or drawn in public places
Pigment	natural colouring matter made of animal or plant tissue
Virtual	created by a computer
Welding	join metal parts together by melting the surfaces by heat
Moulding	forming an object out of material that can be shaped
Casting	object made by pouring hot liquid into a container and leaving it to become solid
Percussion instrument	musical instrument like a drum sounded by striking or shaking
Pantomime	art or technique of conveying emotions, actions, and feelings by gestures
Animated	films and drawings that have been created by a computer and shows them moving

ANSWERS

Page 30. Activity 1

This was far too easy for you to be looking for the answers.

Page 31. Activity 3

1. F	2. E	3. G
4. A	5. H	6. D
7. B	8. C	

Page 31. Activity 2

1. Xylophone
2. Drum
3. Guitar
4. Violin
5. Piano